Text: *Vivienne Crow*

Series editor: *Tony Bowerman*

Photographs: *Vivienne Crow, Carl Rogers, National Trust Images/Steven Barber, Lingholm Estate, Beatrix Potter Society, Alamy, Adobe Stock, Dreamstime, Shutterstock*

Design: *Carl Rogers*

Northern Eye Books

ISBN 978-1-908632-46-3

A CIP catalogue record for this book is available from the British Library.

www.northerneyebooks.co.uk

Cover: *Lingholm Kitchen, Portinscale (Walk 8)*

Important Advice: The routes described in this book are undertaken at the reader's own risk. Walkers should take into account their level of fitness, wear suitable footwear and clothing, and carry food and water. It is also advisable to take the relevant OS map with you in case you get lost and leave the area covered by our maps.

Whilst every care has been taken to ensure the accuracy of the route directions, the publishers cannot accept responsibility for errors or omissions, or for changes in the details given. Nor can the publisher and copyright owners accept responsibility for any consequences arising from the use of this book.

Food images are for illustration purposes only and are not necessarily available at specific locations.

If you find any inaccuracies in either the text or maps, please either write to us or email us at the addresses below. Thank you.

First published in 2018 by:

Northern Eye Books Limited

Northern Eye Books, Tattenhall, Cheshire CH3 9PX

Email: tony@northerneyebooks.com

For sales enquiries, please call 01928 723 744

Twitter: @viviennecrow2
@Northerneyeboo
@Top10walks

Contents

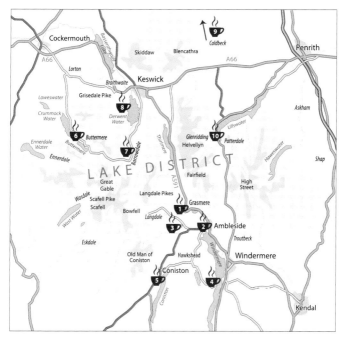

England's Largest National Park

THE LAKE DISTRICT NATIONAL PARK is the largest and most popular of the thirteen National Parks in England and Wales. Created as one of Britain's first National Parks in 1951, its role is to 'conserve and enhance' the natural beauty, wildlife and culture of this iconic English landscape, not just for residents and visitors today but for future generations, too.

Remarkably, the National Park contains every scrap of England's land over 3,000 feet, including its highest mountain, Scafell Pike. Packed within the Park's 912 square miles are numerous peaks and fells, over 400 lakes and tarns, around 50 dales, eight National Nature Reserves, and more than 100 Sites of Special Scientific Interest — all publicly accessible on nearly 2,000 miles of footpaths and other rights of way. It's no surprise then, that the Lake District attracts an estimated 15 million visitors a year.

The Lake District fells reflected in the mirror-like calm of Buttermere

Cafés, Tea Shops and Bistros

A visit to a tea shop adds something special to a walk. It's always a treat to sit down to coffee and cake at the end of an afternoon stroll or to tuck into a hearty lunch half-way through a gorgeous hike.

From quaint little tea rooms that still serve drinks in china cups to modern cafés staffed by trained baristas, the Lake District has plenty to offer — and all surrounded by a truly breathtaking UNESCO World Heritage landscape.

Surely everyone's cup of tea.

"Yes, that's it," said the Hatter with a sigh, "It's always tea time..."

Lewis Carroll

TOP 10 Walks: Cafés, Tea Shops and Bistros

THE TEN TEA SHOPS IN THIS BOOK have been chosen partly on the basis of the excellent walking that can be enjoyed from their doors, and partly on the basis of the fare and ambience they have to offer.

They occupy village, lakeside and woodland locations. The walks themselves take in hidden valleys, low fells, lakes, waterfalls, riverside paths, fabulous viewpoints and wildflower-filled woods — a tremendous array of the sort of scenery for which the Lake District has become world famous.

Brew at Heidi's, Grasmere — page 8

The Rattle Ghyll, Ambleside — page 14

Elterwater Café, Elterwater — page 18

Cafe in the Courtyard, Claife — page 24

Brew at Heidi's is located in the centre of the village of Grasmere

Brew at Heidi's

A walk on to a fell topped by fascinating rock formations, the steep climb rewarded by grand views

What to expect:
Valley lanes and tracks; mostly clear paths on fell; steep ascent and descent

Distance/time: 7.5 kilometres/ 4½ miles. Allow 2¾-3¼ hours

Start: Brew at Heidi's Grasmere Lodge, Red Lion Square, Grasmere (park in one of the village's pay-and-display car parks)

Grid ref: NY 336 074

Ordnance Survey Map: Explorer OL7 The English Lakes Southeastern area, *Windermere, Kendal & Silverdale*

Café: Brew at Heidi's Grasmere Lodge, Red Lion Square, Grasmere LA22 9SP | 015394 35248 | www.heidisgrasmerelodge.co.uk

Walk outline: Helm Crag stands like a sentry above Grasmere, its distinctive summit rocks attracting the eye of motorists as they drive along the A591. This walk ascends the well-used path from the Easedale end of the village, enjoying spectacular views from both sides of the ridge. It then descends by a zig-zagging path to Greenburn, a peaceful side valley that sees few visitors. From here, quiet lanes lead back to Grasmere.

An array of mouth-watering cakes greets you as you walk into Brew, but there's plenty more on offer here including pasties, sandwiches and hot meals. The staff will also prepare packed lunches if you're going to be out all day.

Fancy a brew?

▶ Brew at a glance

Open: Daily, 9am-5pm

Food and specialities: Brew serves sandwiches, pasties and homemade hot meals, including house specialities the Mega Breakfast and Smoked Cheese on Toast. A children's menu is also available.

Beverages: Illy coffee, Brew tea, soft drinks and a range of local speciality beers and spirits

Outside: You'll find a handful of tables in front of the café

Dogs: Well-behaved dogs are welcome and are always offered a treat

The Walk

1. With your back to the entrance to **Brew**, turn left along the road. When it bends right, take the lane straight ahead. (A sign indicates this is the lane leading up to 'Allan Bank'; it's not Langdale Road.) Just after a **cattle grid**, take the path on the right

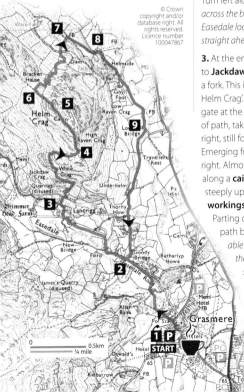

— signposted 'Goody Bridge'. *You'll see Helm Crag straight ahead now, looking impossibly steep from here. Don't be put off — the path that climbs the fell takes a zig-zagging route, making life a little easier for walkers.*

2. The path ends at a gate, which leads on to **Easedale Road** at **Goody Bridge**. Turn left along this. *As you head out across the broad valley bottom, the fells of Easedale loom large, including Tarn Crag straight ahead.*

3. At the end of the public road — close to **Jackdaw Cottage** — bear right at a fork. This is signposted 'Far Easedale, Helm Crag'. A few metres beyond the gate at the top of the cobbled section of path, take the **walled path** on the right, still following signs for 'Helm Crag'. Emerging from between the walls, turn right. Almost immediately, bear left along a **cairned path** heading fairly steeply uphill through **old quarry workings** and then beside a wall. Parting company with the wall, the path bends sharp left. *You're soon able to look up into Easedale with the white streak of Sourmilk Gill slicing through the bedrock to the west.* There are other paths on to Helm Crag, but try to keep to the **constructed path** as much as possible: not only are you

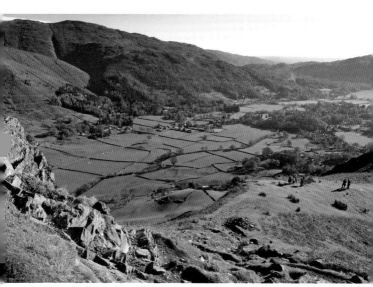

Nearly there: *Looking down on Grasmere from the final climb on to Helm Crag*

helping reduce erosion on this popular fellside, but, doing it this way makes the sudden appearance of Fairfield, to the east, all the more dramatic. When the constructed path ends, keep to the widest route ahead to reach the ridge and that impressive view of the fells on the other side of the valley, including Fairfield.

4. Swing left to continue the climb. You soon encounter a fork in the path. The left-hand route is the easier option, missing out the straightforward scrambling up to the **Lion and the Lamb**. But the right-hand option is more interesting because it gives you a chance to look down on the fascinating jumble of shattered rocks to the east of the ridge. Beyond this first group of rocks, the paths converge for the final climb towards the **highest rocks on the ridge — the so-called Howitzer**.

Helm Crag is one of 214 peaks in the Lake District listed in Alfred Wainwright's Pictorial Guides to the Lakeland Fells. They are now collectively known as the

Cannon fodder?: *The distinctive summit rock on Helm Crag is called the Howitzer*

Wainwrights, much beloved of peak-baggers who aim to climb them all. Strictly speaking though, Helm Crag is the only Wainwright that Wainwright himself never climbed. Although he reached the summit area, the tricky rocks of the Howitzer, the highest point on the fell, defeated him.

5. From the summit, the path drops steeply into a dip on the ridge.

6. Before it begins climbing again, take the narrow trail descending through the bracken on the right. This soon zig-zags down into **Greenburn**, making light work of what would be a steep descent.

Don't be lured off course by any of the sheep trods on the bends. After crossing a stile, head straight down the grassy slope before swinging right to resume your zig-zagging descent. After two gates in quick succession, continue down the grassy slope. The path isn't obvious at first, but soon becomes clearer.

7. Cross the **wooden bridge** over the beck. At the top of the steps on the other side, turn right along the track. Go through the gate and, when the wall on your right ends, go through the gate over to the left.

8. Join the **surfaced lane** heading downhill and turn right at the T-junction.

9. Take the next road on the right — just before the **bridge over the River Rothay**. This eventually brings you back out on to the **Easedale Road** just above **Goody Bridge**. Turn left and then go through the gate on your right to start retracing your route into **Grasmere** village. Remember to keep left at a waymarked junction just after a kissing-gate and then turn left on reaching **Allan Bank's driveway** to complete the walk. ♦

William Wordsworth

The words Grasmere and Wordsworth are forever entwined. The Romantic poet lived in the village for many years and is buried, along with family members, in the graveyard of St Oswald's Church. The walk passes close to Allan Bank, one of his many homes, but not his favourite. He had originally condemned the Georgian house as an eyesore when it was first built. He lived there for just two years.

The Rattle Ghyll is hidden in a little alley in Ambleside

The Rattle Ghyll

A short stroll into a beautiful side valley hemmed in by the high fells

What to expect:
Mostly good valley tracks and paths; old bridge without parapets

---

Distance/time: 5 kilometres/ 3 miles. Allow 1¾ – 2 hours

Start: The Rattle Ghyll, Ambleside (park in one of the village's pay-and-display car parks)

Grid ref: NY 376 045

Ordnance Survey Map: Explorer OL7 The English Lakes South-eastern area, *Windermere, Kendal & Silverdale*

Café: The Rattle Ghyll, Bridge Street, Ambleside LA22 9DU | 015394 31321 | www.rattleghyll.com

---

Walk outline: Despite having a clear track running through it, the narrow valley of Scandale has a surprisingly wild feel. Using quiet lanes and the track, this short stroll heads out along the wooded east bank of Scandale Beck to give a tiny taste of the dale. About half-way into the walk, the return route begins by crossing the humpback High Sweden Bridge. On more open ground now, there are uninterrupted views of Windermere.

There's always a warm welcome in the cosy Rattle Ghyll. Tucked away in a quiet Ambleside alley, it serves up tasty, meat-free fare, including a popular chilli full of pulses and vegetables. All food is made on the premises except the bread from a local bakery.

Mmm, cakes

▶ **The Rattle Ghyll at a glance**

Open: Wed-Sun, 10am-4pm

Food and Specialities: Wholesome soups, platters and sandwiches — all meat-free. Smaller portions for children. Gluten-free bread available. For the sweet-toothed, try the tasting plate of five cakes, ideal for sharing.

Beverages: Teas and coffee from local suppliers; soft drinks including real fruit smoothies

Outside: There are a few tables in front of the café

Dogs: Well-behaved dogs welcome

The Walk

1. With your back to the café, head up to the right and then turn left along the lane. At a T-junction, turn right and take the next road on the left — **Sweden Bridge Lane**. The lane makes its way steadily uphill. As Belle Vue Lane goes left, keep right.

2. Bear left at the next fork, staying with Sweden Bridge Lane. Ignoring a path to the right, you go through a gate. The lane has now become a rough track.

Patches of woodland make this route particularly

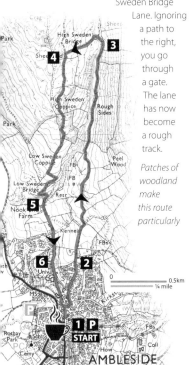

vibrant in spring when the trees are regaining their leaves and the slopes are adorned with bluebells and wild garlic. As the track climbs, Scandale Beck makes it presence felt: first as a gently flowing stream, then as a surging torrent cascading down through a more constricted, rocky gorge.

3. Beyond the woods, keep left at a fork, following a narrow path beside the beck. Like many packhorse bridges, **High Sweden Bridge** doesn't have parapets so you'll need to keep hold of young children as you cross it. *The name Sweden, which crops up several times in the lower reaches of Scandale, is thought to be a corruption of the dialect word 'swithen', meaning land cleared by burning.* Once over the beck, go through the first gate and then bear left to go through a second. A **pitched path** ascends beside a wall and fence.

4. Soon after a **ladder stile**, a broad, stony track is reached. Bear left along this. Just before it swings left, you get one last chance to enjoy a final glimpse of upper Scandale. Then, after passing through a wall gap and cresting a short rise, the views are dominated by Windermere. Keep straight ahead when the stony track goes through a gate on the right.

No railings: *A walker crosses the ancient arch of High Sweden Bridge*

5. Scandale Beck is recrossed via **Low Sweden Bridge**. Here, the beck comes tumbling down through a rocky, wooded ravine. The rough track passes through the yard of **Nook End Farm** and then becomes a surfaced lane.

6. At a three-way junction, take the middle option — straight ahead and continuing downhill. Just after another lane joins from the left, you reach a T-junction. Turn left and immediately right. You'll find **The Rattle Ghyll** down a little alley on your right in about 100 metres (signposted 'Footpath to Rydal Road'), to complete the walk. ♦

Packhorse bridges

Cumbria is criss-crossed by dozens of ancient routes once used by packhorse trains to transport goods such as wool, slate, timber and even lead. These became a common sight from roughly the thirteenth century onwards Sturdy fell ponies would often carry huge, bulky loads. That's why many of the bridges on these routes, including High Sweden Bridge, didn't have parapets — to allow the ponies to pass unhindered.

Elterwater Café is a welcome retreat for walkers

Elterwater Café

A straightforward linear valley stroll surrounded by magnificent mountain scenery

What to expect:
Largely on good valley paths; route less clear on final stretch

Distance/time: 8.5 kilometres/ 5¼ miles. Allow 2¾-3¼ hours
Start: Roadside parking on B5343 close to its junction with A593 at Skelwith Bridge. **Grid ref:** SN 107 147
Finish: Bus stop at entrance to Old Dungeon Ghyll Hotel. **Grid ref:** NY 285 059
Ordnance Survey Map: Explorer OL6 The English Lakes South-western area, *Coniston, Ulverston & Barrow-in-Furness* AND OL7 The English Lakes South-eastern area, *Windermere, Kendal & Silverdale*
Café: Elterwater Café, Elterwater LA22 9HP | 015394 37755

Walk outline: If you're looking for easy walking in spectacular surroundings, look no further. Starting from Skelwith Bridge near Ambleside and with the majestic Langdale Pikes dominating the scene for much of the time, this linear route makes its way up into Great Langdale using lanes, tracks and trails. It ends at the Old Dungeon Ghyll Hotel, from where walkers can catch the No. 516 bus back to Skelwith Bridge.

Small but perfectly formed, the Elterwater Café offers simple options for walkers looking for rest and refreshment. The friendly staff cater for early birds with croissants and a variety of tasty breakfast baps. There are lunches too as well as a wide range of cakes, scones and tray bakes.

Friendly staff

▶ **Elterwater Café at a glance**

Open: Daily, 9.30am-4.30pm, but closed Tues, Thurs and Sun in winter
Food and specialities: Breakfast menu includes croissants, crumpets, filled baps and scrambled egg on toast. For lunch, there are sandwiches, toasties, baked potatoes and soup. Gluten-free options available. English Lakes ice-cream
Beverages: Hot drinks, including Suki pyramid teas; variety of soft drinks
Outside: A few tables outside
Dogs: Well-behaved dogs welcome

The Walk

1. Walk east along the **B5343** to its junction with the **A593**. Turn right and then turn right along the driveway leading up to **Chesters by the River**. When the lane forks, bear right. The path passes between the **old quarry workshops**, then upstream beside the **River Brathay**. Watch for **Skelwith Force**, small by Lakeland standards — but an impressive sight after heavy rain. Keeping the water on your left all the time, the path heads out across meadows and past **Elterwater**.

2. Eventually, the popular path leads into the **National Trust car park** at **Elterwater village**.

Elterwater developed as an industrial settlement based on quarrying and the manufacture of gunpowder. To ensure a constant and reliable water supply, Stickle Tarn, high above the valley, was dammed. Charcoal was supplied by the local alder coppices, while sulphur and saltpetre were imported from abroad. By the start of the 20th century, the works employed about 80 people, known as 'powder monkeys'.

On reaching the road, turn right for 70 metres to visit **Elterwater Café**, or, to continue on the main route, turn left and immediately right. Follow this quarry access lane for 360 metres and then take the clearly marked footpath dropping to the right — signposted Chapel Stile and Great Langdale. At a stone bench next to **Great Langdale Beck**, bear right and cross the **footbridge**.

3. Turn left along the **B5343**. (*Those who want to cut the walk short can continue along the road into Chapel Stile to catch the bus back to Skelwith Bridge.*)

Tranquil scene: *Elterwater with the distinctive Langdale Pikes in the background*

To continue on the main walk, take the stony path on the left just after the **Wainwrights' Inn** — signposted Baysbrown campsite. At a surfaced lane, turn left and then bear right along a walled track. Keep left at the next footpath junction — close to the edge of **Chapel Stile**.

4. After crossing **New Bridge**, the track follows **Great Langdale Beck** upstream. At the next **bridge**, it swings up to the left. Just behind the buildings at **Oak Howe**, keep right at a fork — signposted 'New Dungeon Ghyll'. *From New Bridge onwards, the Langdale Pikes dominate the scene ahead. They loom imperiously over their eponymous valley, Harrison Stickle is the most haughty of the bunch, seemingly*

Serene scene: *Great Langdale Beck tumbles through the woods in early autumn*

well aware of its status as a Lake District icon. Eventually, Crinkle Crags and Bow Fell also appear at the head of the valley. The path climbs to cross a **beck** and then goes through a gap in a wall before descending towards **Side House**.

5. Do not cross the bridge just before the buildings here; instead, follow the **beck** upstream for another 45 metres and then cross the **bridge** and **ladder stile** on your right. A narrow but clear path contours the hillside and leads to a second ladder stile. Continue along the faint trail and through a **kissing-gate.**

6. On nearing a wall, go through the gate on the right to descend through the trees. After the next gate, swing half-right down the grassy slope to pass through a **gap in a wall**. You'll soon enter the **National Trust's Great Langdale campsite**. *The National Trust owns or manages most of Langdale: a wide-ranging portfolio that includes almost all of the fells on either side of the valley, two pubs, a campsite and several farms. Its relationship with Langdale dates back to 1929 when the wealthy historian, George Macaulay Trevelyan, gifted the Old Dungeon Ghyll Hotel and 50 acres of adjoining land to the National Trust.* Continue in the same direction, making

for a wall corner and then walk with the wall on your left, soon crossing a **footbridge**. Turn left along the track and leave the campsite via a gate.

7. Turn right along the road and follow it round a sharp bend to the right. The turning on the left in another 65 metres leads to the **Old Dungeon Ghyll Hotel**. Catch the No. 516 bus back to Skelwith Bridge from this junction to complete the walk. ♦

Swan Lake?

Elterwater is said to mean 'lake of the swan'. Mute swans live here all year round and, in the winter, the lake is home to over-wintering whooper swans. Flying up to 1,400 kilometres between Iceland and the British Isles, whooper swans make what is believed to be the longest sea crossing of any swan species. These huge birds mate for life and their cygnets stay with them throughout the winter migration.

Welcome
to
Cafe in the Courtyard
Homemade Pies,
Cakes, Soups &
toasties 10am
4·30 PM
OPEN everyday

The Café in the Courtyard is situated close to the shores of Windermere

Café in the Courtyard,

Woodland and lakeside walking on Windermere's western shore

What to expect:
Woodland trails, indistinct in places; good tracks; quiet lanes; fields; lakeshore

Distance/time: 10 kilometres/ 6 miles. Allow 3-3½ hours

Start: Small National Trust car park, 400 metres south-west of the Ferry House on the B5285. This car park is located beside the road; it's not the one signposted to the right after you come off the ferry

Grid ref: SD 387 954

Ordnance Survey Map: Explorer OL7 The English Lakes South-eastern area, *Windermere, Kendal & Silverdale*

Café: Café in the Courtyard, Claife Viewing Station, near Far Sawrey, Hawkshead LA22 0LW | www.nationaltrust.org.uk

Walk outline: This lovely walk starts with a visit to the restored Claife Viewing Station before climbing through towering woodland. Snatched glimpses of the lake appear through the trees before the route drops into Far Sawrey. From here, we slowly descend to the shores of Windermere south of Cunsey. A relaxing lakeside path then heads north in the company of geese, swans and people messing about on the water.

A stone's throw from the shores of Windermere, this café occupies an enclosed courtyard just below Claife Viewing Station. It's a no-frills place and food is served in recyclable cardboard containers. Try the ferryman's lunch, the lakeside equivalent of a ploughman's.

Stunning lake views

▶ Café in the Courtyard at a glance

Open: Daily, 10.30am-4pm (winter 11am-3pm)

Food and specialities: Serves a selection of locally made pies, sausage rolls and cakes, including the café's own Sawrey pie. Any items on the menu can be adapted for children

Beverages: Soft drinks; locally supplied hot beverages including coffee from Cumbrian roaster Carvetti. Café's baristas fully trained by Carvetti

Outside: Large courtyard with several tables

Dogs: Dogs welcome and waggy tails receive a free treat

The Walk

1. Take the broad path near the back of the **car park**. It has a low, wooden barrier across it and is signposted to the 'Claife Viewing Station and ferry'. Turn left to climb the steps and then left again at the top (or right to visit the **café**). You'll see the **viewing station** immediately in front of you. Having explored it, continue on the path through the **archway** and then swing left up through a gap in the rocks. The path now begins climbing through **Station Scar Wood** where giant ferns litter the forest floor. A section of steep switchbacks leads up on to **Mitchell Knotts**, where you bear right. Soon walking with a fence on your left, glimpses of Windermere come and go through the tall trees. *On a sunny day, even Bowness-on-Windermere looks attractive from up here.* The narrow path can be muddy at times, so watch your footing as it undulates across this bumpy ground.

2. After a small gate, turn left along a walled path — signposted 'Far Sawrey'.

Keep straight on at the next junction of routes — through the gate. As the track begins descending, the Coniston fells appear to the west as does Grizedale Forest. Having teamed up with another track from the right, the route drops past the **Sawrey Institute** to reach the **B5285** at **Far Sawrey**.

Relaxing: *The Café in the Courtyard*

3. Turn right and, almost immediately, take the lane dropping left. This soon joins another lane from the right. Ignore one footpath to the right, but then, just after passing below the **church**, go through the kissing-gate on the right to join a rough track. Bear right to keep to a grassy, parallel track that runs closer to the fence on the right. As the field narrows, you'll see one gate on the right and another to the left. Cross the stile next to the latter and then, in a few more strides, bear right along a faint

track through the grass. One wooden gate is followed quickly by wet ground and a second gate. Once through this, the right-of-way heads straight through the middle of this open area. However, the ground is very wet, so you may find it easier to swing up to the left to bypass any swampiness. On the far side, a gate leads into the trees.

4. A narrow trail now meanders roughly south-west through the **pleasant woods**. This brings you out on to a quiet lane, along which you turn left. Go left again at a T-junction.

Shady shore: *Part of the walk follows a pretty path beside Windermere*

5. About 300 metres along this road — just as it bends right and begins to climb — go through the gate on the left to join a bridleway towards 'Low Cunsey'. At a waymarked fork, bear right and you'll soon head out into an open area used by forestry vehicles. Keep to the main track as it bends left.

6. On dropping to a minor road opposite **Low Cunsey Farm**, turn right. After about 600 metres of road walking, watch for an awkward stile on the left — close to a **barn**. Cross this — signposted 'High Cunsey and Rawlinson Nab'. Before long, the path leads to the edge of **Windermere**. Sometimes you're walking along the stony shore; at other times, you're on a path through the trees that fringe the lake, but you're never more than a few metres from the water's edge. **Rawlinson Nab** itself has a bench: a great place to stop and enjoy the views across the lake. Just after an **old boathouse**, the route crosses a stile in a wall, partly hidden by the vegetation. It then regains the **lakeshore**. Eventually, on reaching another **boathouse**, the shore path joins a track that swings away from the water.

7. Turn right along a quiet lane. Take the second lane on the right. At a T-junction with the **B5285**, go through the gap in the wall on the right to join an off-road path signposted to the 'ferry'. When you next come out on to the road, cross diagonally right to pick up a path continuing in roughly the same direction but now to the left of the asphalt. This soon drops you back into the **car park** and starting point to complete the walk. ♦

Through rose-tinted glass?

Claife Viewing Station was built in the 1790s when the 'Picturesque' movement was at its height. Early tourists came here to admire the lakeside landscape. With the woods restricting the view as they climbed, there would be a 'grand reveal' at the top. The windows were tinted to give visitors an idea of how the scenery looked in different conditions: orange for autumn and dark blue for moonlight, for example.

There's just a small beach between the Bluebird Café and Coniston Water

Bluebird Café

Easy walking along a disused railway with a leisurely return on an attractive lake shore path

What to expect:
Disused railway; fields; walled tracks; roadside paths; woodland trails; lakeshore

Distance/time: 9 kilometres/ 5½ miles. Allow 2½-3 hours

Start: Lake District National Park's Coniston Boating Centre car park at end of Lake Road, Coniston

Grid ref: SD 308 971

Ordnance Survey Map: OS Explorer OL6 The English Lakes South-western area, *Coniston, Ulverston & Barrow-in-Furness*

Café: Bluebird Café, Lake Road, Coniston LA21 8AN | 015394 41649 | www.thebluebirdcafe.co.uk

Walk outline: Starting from the lakeshore, this walk skirts the edge of Coniston to join a permissive path along a disused railway. Having followed this south, it then heads out across fields and through woodland to reach the western shore of Coniston Water. We now enjoy an easy, waterside stroll north in tranquil surroundings — in and out of the trees and with some fantastic views of the craggy fells looming over the village.

You can't get closer to the lake than this smashing little café. Step up from Coniston Water's shingle beach and on to an outside seating area with good protection from the elements all-year round. The comfortable interior gets very busy at weekends.

Lakeside café

▶ Bluebird Café at a glance

Open: Daily, 9.30am-5.30pm, May-Sept (shorter opening, Oct-April)
Food and Specialities: As well as a wide range of sandwiches and jacket potatoes, the Bluebird serves pasta meals and a variety of different salads. Also daily specials and cakes
Beverages: As well as the usual refreshments, the café sells wine, beer and some spirits
Outside: Sheltered seating area
Dogs: Dogs welcome in outside seating area only

The Walk

1. From the car park, walk back up **Lake Road** for about 180 metres and then cross the **footbridge** on the left — signed to 'Coniston'. A path briefly follows the beck upstream to the **car park of the Lake Road commercial estate**. Cross the parking area, heading for the vehicle exit, and then turn right along the access lane.

2. At the next junction, take the **cycle path to Torver** on the left. You'll encounter more of this path later in the walk but, for now, follow it for only 80 metres and then go through the double gate on the right. You're now standing next to the **school playing fields**. Go through a gate about 30 metres to your left. This provides access to an enclosed grassy path which, in turn, leads to a surfaced lane.

Follow this to the main road and carefully cross over to take the narrow lane opposite. As this winds its way steeply uphill, keep left when a driveway goes right.

3. About 150 metres beyond the main road, as the lane performs a sharp left bend, go through the gap in the wall to the right of the asphalt. You are now standing on the **trackbed of the Coniston branch line**

of the former Furness Railway. Turn left. As you'd expect of a disused railway, the next stretch of the route is very straightforward and requires minimal effort, allowing you to appreciate the woods and occasional glimpses of the lake. After almost 900 metres, the permitted path ends at a lane.

4. Turn left and then go right along the **A593**. After about 65 metres, go through the gate on the left

Waterside wanderer: *Walking on the lakeside path beside Coniston Water*

— signed 'Torver'. Picking up the route of the **old railway** again, the path runs along the bottom of a shallow ditch. Soon after two gates in quick succession, bear right along **Park Coppice caravan site**'s access lane. When this swings right, take the clear path to the left of the bend, soon going through a small gate. When this ends, go through the gate on the right and then turn left along a path running parallel with the A593. (You have a wall between you and the road at first, but this later disappears.)

5. This roadside path later drops through a gate on the left. Before long, you're walking another section of the railway that's been converted to path. Follow the **old railway** under the **bridge** and for a further 300 metres — until you reach a fingerpost at a path crossing.

6. Go through the gate on the left here — signed 'Coniston Water'. Cross the tumbledown wall directly in front

Victorian engineering: *The National Trust's steam yacht* Gondola *on Coniston Water*

of you and head half-left across the open area to a gate and stile at the top of a slope. Cross the stile and take the fenced track climbing on the other side of the surfaced lane — signed 'Torver Jetty'. When the route splits, take the branch on the right. Having passed through a few gates, the clear, stony path comes to an abrupt end. Aim for the dip in the woods below you and the path will reappear. It enters **Torver Common Wood** and, before long, you'll see Coniston Water glinting through the trees ahead.

7. Go left at the water's edge, soon passing **Torver Jetty**. Immediately after the gate just beyond the jetty of Birmingham University's boating centre, bear right, soon passing through another gate to regain the **lakeshore**. An open, grassy area provides magnificent views of the Coniston Fells, and John Ruskin's former home Brantwood can be seen on the other side of the lake. When a clear path leads to a surfaced track, bear right. Beyond a **red-and-white barrier**, this passes to the immediate left of **Coniston Hall**, a 16th-century house with distinctive cylindrical chimneys.

8. Beyond a gate between two stone **farm buildings**, turn right along a gravel path. This ends close to the **Lake Road Estate**. Retracing your steps from earlier, turn right along the access lane — signed 'Coniston Pier'. Remember to turn left into the commercial estate's car park and then right after the bridge to return to the **car park** and **café** to complete the walk. ♦

Bluebird K7

Bluebird K7 was the name of the speed boat in which Donald Campbell attempted his world water-speed record. He'd already achieved a record-breaking 276.33mph in Australia in 1964, but he wanted to break the 300mph barrier. While attempting this on Coniston Water in January 1967, his vehicle slowly lifted out of the water, did a backward somersault in the air and then plummeted into the lake nose first, killing Campbell instantly.

Relaxing at a sunny table outdoors

Croft House Farm Café

A varied walk taking in a lake side path, a hidden valley and a low ridge with magnificent views

What to expect:
Fields, woodland and lakeshore paths and ascent of low fell

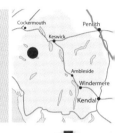

Distance/time: 8 kilometres/ 5 miles. Allow 3-3½ hours
Start: Lake District National Park car park in Buttermere (behind Bridge Hotel)
Grid ref: NY 173 169
Ordnance Survey Map: OL4 The English Lakes North-western area, *Keswick, Cockermouth & Wigton*
Café: Croft House Farm Café, Buttermere CA13 9XA | 017687 70235 www.crofthousefarmcafe.co.uk

Walk outline: After a brief stroll beside Crummock Water, this walk climbs part way up Rannerdale Knotts' southern slopes for superb views across the lake. Having dropped back to lake level, it then climbs through serene and secluded Rannerdale. A delightful, grassy ridge then leads out to the 355 metre top of Rannerdale Knotts, a whipper-snapper of a fell that can hold its own in this land of giants. The return is via a wooded ravine.

Whatever the weather, the Croft House Farm Café is always bustling with walkers. They come in anticipation, not of gourmet food, but of simple lunches and warming drinks — or, in hot weather, delicious English Lakes Ice Cream. The café also has a small shop selling maps, guidebooks and some groceries.

Tempting menu board

▶ Croft House Farm Café at a glance

Open: Daily, 10am-5pm
Food and specialities: Basic lunches including sandwiches, panini, jacket potatoes and soup. All sandwiches and panini are made fresh each morning and wrapped to be taken away or eaten in.
Beverages: Hot and cold drinks, including the cafe's own butterbeer — a caramel fudge drink
Outside: Several tables outside the café
Dogs: Dogs welcome in outside seating area only

The Walk

1. Walk to the far end of the **car park**, away from the vehicle entrance. Ignoring the large gates, go through a **small wooden gate** over to the right. This provides access to a **beckside path**. Don't be tempted by the bridge leading into the campsite early on; keep the water on your right for now.

2. Cross the **beck** via the **next bridge** and turn left through the woods. The trail swings right, keeping close to the wall on the left. Go through the next **kissing-gate in the wall** and then follow the fence on your right down to the edge of **Crummock Water**. Turn right through the gate and over the **bridge**. Bear left at a fork to keep to the gorgeous **lakeshore path** through the trees. Leaving the woods via another gate, head back to the water's edge and then make for the small **stand of pine trees** near the base of the fell.

3. Climb to the road immediately after a gate among these trees. Cross straight over the asphalt and climb the grassy trail opposite to reach a wide path, along which you bear left. This gently rising route cuts a green swathe through the bracken, running almost parallel with the south-east shore of Crummock Water and providing superb views of the fells across the water. Ignoring any trails to the right, keep to the broad path and you will eventually reach a point where you can see down to the northern end of the lake.

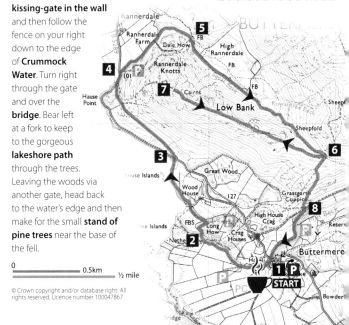

0 _____ 0.5km
_____ ½ mile

Hidden valley: *Looking back down High Rannerdale to Crummock Water*

The way ahead is a little less clear now: ignoring the trail uphill to the right, swing slightly left over the damp ground to begin descending. An obvious path quickly materialises.

4. On reaching the road, turn right and then, in a few more metres, right again into a gravel **parking area**. Walking with a wall on your left, follow the path around the craggy, western base of **Rannerdale Knotts**. After a **small**

gate, *you enter an area that is awash with bluebells in the spring.* Keep right at any forks to reach the beck – known as **Rannerdale Beck** at this point. Walk upstream with the beck on your left.

5. On reaching a **footbridge** over the beck, don't cross; instead, go through the gate in the wall on your right and continue upstream. The climb through this peaceful valley is gentle at first, but becomes a little steeper the higher you get. Nearing the head of the dale, ignore a trail heading more steeply uphill to the left.

Sunrise sublime: *The low dawn sun highlights mist over Crummock Water*

6. A few metres further on, swing slightly right to stand at a junction of paths with a fine view across to Red Pike and the High Stile range. You'll return to this point later in the walk but, for now, turn sharp right along the **rising ridge path**. Known as **Low Bank**, this splendid ridge is surprisingly narrow for such a small fell, but never intimidating. You can follow it out as far as you wish, but eventually you will have to retrace your steps. The highest point on **Rannerdale Knotts**, at the far north-western end of the ridge, is marked by a **small cairn**.

The path undulates on its journey west and there is one rocky section.

7. When you do finally turn round and head back the way you came, make sure you stay on the main ridge path — there are trails off to the right and left. On returning to the junction at the south-eastern end of the ridge (at waypoint six), turn right. As you descend, keep left at any obvious forks and junctions. You'll head south-west at first, but quickly swing south-south-west. About 350 metres after leaving the ridge, a crossing of grassy paths is reached. This is just above a sumptuous **oak woodland**. Turn left here to drop towards the trees.

8. Enter the woods via a gate and a set of steps. The path swings right to head downstream with **Mill Beck**. There are steep drops down into the gill in places, so watch your footing. Turn left at the road and immediately right, beside the **Bridge Hotel**. Bear right in front of **The Fish Inn** to re-enter the car park, to complete the walk. ♦

Bluebells under threat

The British bluebell is usually found in woodland, but in Rannerdale it grows on the open valley floor. This native plant is under threat in the UK from the Spanish bluebell, imported into our gardens by the Victorians. It's easy to tell them apart: the top of the stem of the native British bluebell droops like a shepherd's crook, while the Spanish bluebell has a straight stem. Unfortunately, the two have crossbred in the wild.

Walkers enjoying outdoor refreshments at the Flock In

ROSTHWAITE

Flock In

Woodland and beckside walking at its very best in the iconic Borrowdale valley

What to expect:
Good tracks; riverside and woodland paths; fields; roads; one wet section

---

Distance/time: 10 kilometres/ 6½ miles. Allow 2¾-3¾ hours

Start: National Trust car park in Rosthwaite, Borrowdale

Grid ref: NY 257 148

Ordnance Survey Map: Explorer OL4 The English Lakes North-western area, *Keswick, Cockermouth & Wigton*

Teashop: Flock In tearoom, Yew Tree Farm, Rosthwaite CA12 5XB | 017687 77675 | www.borrowdaleyewtreefarm.co.uk

Walk outline: After following the crystal clear waters of the River Derwent upstream, this walk enters Johnny Wood, climbing slightly and enjoying glimpses of the high fells through the trees. The route passes close to Seatoller, crosses back over the River Derwent and then heads for the tiny hamlet of Stonethwaite. There's an optional short cut here, or you can continue further into the side valley of Langstrath.

Located on a working farm in the heart of this beautiful valley, the Flock In is a cosy tearoom with a relaxed atmosphere. It's probably best known for the dishes made using the farm's own award-winning Herdwick meat, including pasties and stews.

'The walkers' tearoom'

▶ The Flock In at a glance

Open: Thursday-Tuesday, 10am-5pm (closed mid-Nov to early Feb)

Food and specialities: Traditional, hearty grub is on the menu at this cosy tearoom in a converted barn. Simple, hot meals as well as sandwiches and cakes. All home-made

Beverages: Hot and cold drinks

Outside: Outside benches and small garden with tables, some under cover

Dogs: Dogs welcome in outside seating area only

The Walk

1. From the car park entrance, turn right along the lane, soon passing between **Yew Tree Farm** and the **Flock In tearoom**. A walled track leads between the fields of the valley floor. Reaching the **River Derwent**, the walls are lost. Sure-footed walkers might want to cross the **stepping stones** here to reach the west bank, but it's much easier simply to continue along the **cobbled track** beside the river and use **New Bridge**.

2. Having crossed, turn left, quickly crossing a **footbridge** over a tributary beck. At **Longthwaite**, join a surfaced lane heading right. Just before the **'Welcome to Borrowdale YHA' sign**, walk across the grass on the right, keeping fairly close to the wall. A gate provides access to a clear path skirting the edge of **Johnny Wood**. Having followed this for almost 220 metres, go through a small gate on the left.

3. A faint path heads towards the trees and then climbs the wooded slope via a series of zig-zags, negotiating some bare rock along the way. The gradient eases beyond a gap in a wall. As the ground then levels off, don't be tempted by a narrow trail dropping left. *The head of Borrowdale, including Base Brown and the fearsome north-east face of Great End, can be glimpsed through occasional gaps in the trees.* A gate leads out of the woods. Keep straight ahead at a crossing of paths to drop through a second gate.

4. Reaching a wall at a path junction, turn left. After a kissing-gate, the trail passes through a lightly **wooded area**. Emerging from the trees again, about 230 metres beyond the **kissing-gate**, you'll see **Folly Bridge** down to the right.

0   1km
                    1 mile

Autumn colour: *The season of mists and mellow fruitfulness comes to Borrowdale*

To reach this, leave the path just before it passes through a gap in a low wall. Bear right here, heading downhill on a faint, grassy path — with the wall on your immediate left at first. Having crossed the **bridge**, keep close to the fence on your right and then follow the lane to the **Borrowdale road**. Turn left.

5. Having walked the roadside path for about 450 metres, go through the kissing-gate on the right — signed 'Stonethwaite road'. This is the second signposted footpath on the right. A faint grassy track heads straight towards the fells before swinging left. At a wall, turn left — signed '**Chapel House Farm**'. Walk through the **farmyard** and past the little **whitewashed church**.

Turn right at a T-junction.

6. When the road bends right in the hamlet of **Stonethwaite**, you have a choice. (*To cut 3.5 kilometres from the walk's total distance, turn left — signed 'Greenup Edge and Grasmere' — cross*

Enjoying a stroll: *Walking in the mossy woods of Borrowdale*

the bridge over Stonethwaite Beck and then turn left at the T-junction to rejoin the main route at point 9 — signed 'Watendlath via Rosthwaite'.)

To continue on the main route, stay with the lane. Keep right when a track later peels off left into the **campsite**. Drawing close to the noisy waters of **Langstrath Beck**, the track swings right.

7. About 180 metres beyond a gate across the track, use the **footbridge** on your left to reach the far side of the beck. You get one tempting glimpse of

Langstrath from the bridge before you turn left to head downstream again. The path keeps close to the wall and beck on your left. It then goes through a small gate to negotiate a cobbled path nearer the water's edge. After some soggy areas, cross the **bridge over Greenup Gill** — just above where it meets Langstrath Beck to become Stonethwaite Beck.

8. Having crossed, go through the **wooden gate at the top of the steps** and turn left. Keep left at any path junctions or forks.

9. Having walked beside **Stonethwaite Beck** for 1.4 kilometres, you'll see a

signposted track on the left. Those who cut the walk short rejoin the main route here. The route continues downstream beside Stonethwaite Beck for another 1.3 kilometres, the final part of the journey being enclosed by drystone walls. At a junction close to the entrance to **Hazel Bank Hotel**, turn left. Turn left again at the **B5289** and take the lane on the right to return to the **car park** to complete the walk. ♦

Hardy Herdwicks

Borrowdale is full of Herdwicks. These are the hardy native sheep that graze Lakeland's high, exposed fells all year round. The lambs graze with their mothers on the 'heaf' belonging to that farm, which gives them a life-long knowledge of where they should be grazing, a knowledge they will then pass on to their own lambs. The name is thought to come from the Norse, 'herdvyck', meaning sheep pasture.

Lingholm Kitchen is a stylish newcomer to Lakeland's teashop scene

PORTINSCALE

The Lingholm Kitchen

A gentle amble through woods and along a beckside path at the base of the fells

What to expect:
Quiet lanes; beckside path; field paths, woodland tracks and trails

---

Distance/time: 7.5 kilometres/ 4½ miles. Allow 2-2¼ hours

Start: Small car park near Skelgill at base of Cat Bells

Grid ref: NY 245 211

Ordnance Survey Map: OL4 The English Lakes North-western area, *Keswick, Cockermouth & Wigton*

Café: Lingholm Kitchen, Portinscale, near Keswick CA12 5TZ | 017687 71206 | www.thelingholmkitchen.co.uk

---

Walk outline: A lovely beck and sublime fell views are just two of the highlights on this gentle walk in the wooded countryside to the north-west of Derwentwater. After following a gated lane down from Skelgill, you reach Newlands Beck. A beckside path meanders downstream to join quiet lanes and field paths for the walk up to Portinscale. From here, well signposted paths head through the woods skirting the shores of Derwentwater, passing Lingholm Kitchen en route.

Whether it's breakfast, brunch, lunch or afternoon tea, there's always something different on the menu at this modern, airy café. It forms part of the Lingholm Estate and overlooks a Victorian-style walled garden. An onsite bakery makes artisan breads and cakes.

Superb drinks menu

▶ The Lingholm Kitchen at a glance

Open: Daily, 9am-6pm (5pm in winter)

Food and specialities: Hot and cold selections include tasty burgers, a ploughman's lunch, sandwiches and substantial breakfasts — the Huntsman for meat lovers and the Gardener for vegetarians

Beverages: Teas and coffee from local suppliers; cold drinks include craft beers

Outside: Outside seating area at front of café

Dogs: Well-behaved dogs welcome

The Walk

1. With your back to the parking area, turn left along the lane — in the direction of Skelgill. Beyond a gate, the road descends between the buildings at **Skelgill**. Follow it round to the right, soon making directly for Rowling End, Causey Pike and Barrow on the other side of the valley.

2. Turn right at the next road junction and then, after 275 metres, go through the small gate on the left — signed

'Braithwaite'. With **Newlands Beck** keeping you company, this excellent path is followed for about 1.6 kilometres. As the terrain opens out and the beck widens, the scene ahead is dominated by the Skiddaw massif.

3. Turn right when you reach the road and take the turning on the left for 'Ullock'. Having passed all the **buildings at Ullock**, turn left through a pedestrian gate — signed 'Portinscale'. A short section of fenced path leads into a field. Keep to the field edge. After a farm gate, cut straight across the middle of the next field, potentially wet in places. A **gate and bridge** lead on to a shady path heading uphill.

4. Reaching a lane on the edge of **Portinscale**, turn right. Turn right at a T-junction and then, in 250 metres, left along **Nichol End Marine's access lane**.

5. Nearing the **lake**, bear right to pass above the **marina's café**. At a surfaced lane, go left and immediately right.

6. On reaching **Lingholm's driveway**, to visit **Lingholm Kitchen**, go through the gap in the wall on the left and follow the path to the café. To continue on the walk, turn left along the **driveway** and, almost immediately, go through the small gate to the right of the lane. This fenced path passes

Summer inspiration: *Lingholm house where Beatrix Potter sketched in the gardens*

through another stretch of gorgeous **woodland**. Beyond a kissing-gate, you briefly lose the trees. Straight ahead now is Cat Bells, the path up its northern ridge clearly visible. A **gated bridge** provides access to another woodland path leading to a surfaced lane.

7. Cross diagonally left to join a path climbing beside a fence and wall — signed 'Cat Bells and Newlands Valley'. Turn left at the road and then, a few strides beyond the **cattle grid**, take the lane signed to 'Skelgill' on the right. Return to the **car park** ahead on the left to complete the walk. ♦

Beatrix Potter

From 1885 until 1907, the children's writer and conservationist Beatrix Potter used to spend family holidays at Lingholm and Fawe Park on the shores of Derwentwater. Her first book, The Tale of Peter Rabbit, was published during this period as were three more. Many of the illustrations in the books are based on real locations around Derwentwater, including Mr McGregor's garden, based on sketches of Lingholm and Fawe Park.

The Watermill Café occupies an historic, beckside building

CALDBECK

walk 9

Watermill Café

Off-the-beaten-track walk through sylvan countryside to a meeting of two rivers

What to expect:
Woodland and field paths; country lanes

Distance/time: 8.5 kilometres/ 5¼ miles. Allow 2¾ to 3¼ hours

Start: Lake District National Park car park in Caldbeck

Grid ref: NY 323 398

Ordnance Survey Map: OL5 The English Lakes North-eastern area , Penrith, Patterdale & Caldbeck

Café: Watermill Café at Priest's Mill, Caldbeck CA7 8DR | 016974 78267 | www.watermillcafe.co.uk

Walk outline: Wildflower-filled woods, fell views and gorgeous villages are encountered on this stroll in quiet countryside at the base of the Lake District's Northern Fells. It starts from Caldbeck, follows a beck downstream to meet the River Caldew in bluebell woods and then heads to Hesket Newmarket. Country lanes and farm paths then lead back down to Caldbeck via a limestone gorge and dramatic waterfall.

As its name suggests, this café is located in a restored watermill right next to the roaring waters of the village's main beck. Huddle round the wood-burning stove with hot soup on a chilly winter's day; in summer, sit outside in the sheltered garden overlooking Caldbeck's cricket pitch.

A warm welcome

▶ Watermill Café at a glance

Open: Daily, 9am-5pm (winter opening times may differ)
Food and specialities: Generous platters; tart of the day; baked potatoes with various filling; soups, sandwiches, ciabatta. Fairtrade produce. Home-made cakes. Occasional evening openings and roast Sunday lunches.
Beverages: Locally supplied teas and coffees; soft drinks
Outside: Sheltered garden
Dogs: Dogs allowed in garden only
Evenings: Evening acoustic concerts featuring jazz, blues and folk musicians from around the world

The Walk

1. Leave the **car park** via the vehicle entrance (not the exit), cross the road and head down the lane opposite. Watch for the **church** on the other side of the beck — *this is the resting place of nineteenth-century huntsman John Peel, immortalised in the song* D'ye Ken John Peel? (The Watermill Café is on that side of the beck too.) At the lane-end, go through the gate and follow the track to a **water treatment plant**. Head to the right of this — on grass.

2. Go through the next gate close to **Cald Beck** and follow the clearest path at all times (ignore a right fork just before the path begins to rise). Gaining height, it provides great views south towards the Lake District's Northern Fells.

3. About 65 metres after passing through a gate leading on to more open slopes, drop right to cross a stile. Follow the narrow path down through the trees. Cross the **bridge** over **Cald Beck** as it runs through an attractive **gorge**. You're now on a small parcel of woodland cradled between Cald Beck and the River Caldew — almost an island. To get to the point at which the two rivers meet — and to complete a circuit of the 'island' — take the path on the left. (There are several trails here, but as long as you always have a river on your left, you shouldn't go wrong.) The path weaves its way through **bluebell woods** to reach **Watersmeet**, the point at which Cald Beck enters the **River Caldew**. Continue along the river bank, this time with the Caldew on your left.

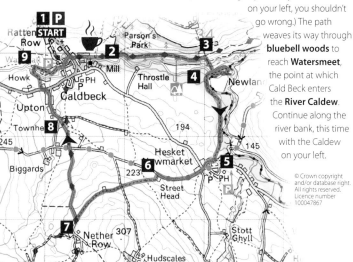

Spring has sprung: *Walking through open woodland near Watersmeet*

4. The trail climbs slightly and reaches a gate close to the **bridge** crossed earlier. Go through the gate and follow the path uphill. Watch for a **kissing-gate** on the left. On the other side of this is another pleasant **woodland trail**. After the next gate, continue in the same direction on a faint path across open ground. A yellow waymarker later indicates the way through another gate and into riverside woodland dominated, in the spring, by wild garlic. A **series of kissing-gates** now leads to a field on the edge of **Hesket Newmarket**. Keep close to the fence on the left. After two gates in quick succession, you come out in the village — opposite the **Old Crown pub**.

5. Turn right, past several pretty **cottages**. At the junction with the main road through the village, turn right. Almost immediately, the road bends right. Leave it here by taking the narrow lane between the **cottages** on the left. After 600 metres, you'll reach the **old farm buildings** of **Street Head**.

Deep purple: *Fragrant bluebells carpet the woodland floor at Watersmeet*

6. Go through the gate on the left on the far side of the **farmhouse**. Beyond the next gate, veer right to cross a stile providing access to a grassy track. At the end of the track, go directly across a large field, aiming for a wooden stile in a section of wall on the far side. Another enclosed path follows. At a junction, go straight across following a farm track.

7. Turn right along a quiet lane just outside the **hamlet of Nether Row**. At a crossroads, go straight over to continue along a very narrow lane.

8. Reaching a junction with a wider road, turn right and follow this to where it splits just before a T-junction. Bear left and left again at the T-junction.

After 100 metres, go through a kissing-gate on the right — signed 'The Howk'. Keep close to the field boundary on the right until the next kissing-gate, providing access to some steps. These descend through the woods to a **bridge over Cald Beck** as it passes through an impressive **limestone gorge**, known as **The Howk**. *This cool, narrow ravine is home to dense vegetation, including the rare shield fern.*

9. Having crossed, climb the **steps** on

the right, follow the path round to the right and then descend some slippery **stone steps** for a better view of **The Howk** and its **waterfall**, a deafening white-water tumult that spirals down through the limestone. The path now leads past a **ruined bobbin mill** and then out, via a yard, to a village lane. Turn left — but not sharp left — and then drop down the track on the right to re-enter the **car park** to complete the walk. ◆

Water power

The Howk was the site of an old bobbin mill which once had a 12.8 metre waterwheel, said to be the largest of its kind in England at the time. Built in 1857, the works closed in 1924. In the middle of the nineteenth century, there were 120 water-powered bobbin mills throughout the Lake District. Between them, they produced about 50 per cent of the world's textile industry bobbins.

Friendly service at the spacious Helvellyn Country Kitchen

GLENRIDDING

Helvellyn Country Kitchen

A fabulous viewpoint above Ullswater and a peaceful beautyspot

What to expect:
Constructed trails; low fell; field path; quiet lanes; roadside path; one ford — avoided by cutting walk short

Distance/time: 6 kilometres/ 4 miles. Allow 1¾-2 hours

Start: Lake District National Park car park in Glenridding

Grid ref: NY 385 169

Ordnance Survey Map: OL5 The English Lakes North-eastern area, *Penrith, Patterdale & Caldbeck*

Café: Helvellyn Country Kitchen, Glenridding CA11 0PA | 01768 482598 | www.helvellynkitchen.co.uk

Walk outline: This walk packs a lot of charm into a short distance. First stop is the pine-topped viewpoint of Keldas, a 311-metre hill commanding an excellent perspective over Ullswater. After a visit to the tree-fringed waters of atmospheric Lanty's Tarn, the route drops into glorious Grisedale. Here, we skirt the base of the fells and ford Hag Beck to reach Patterdale. The walk ends by weaving in and out of the trees as it follows the road back to Glenridding.

This friendly, spacious café is an institution with Glenridding walkers. Tuck into breakfast before heading out or return for a simple lunch after your walk. Bread, cakes and biscuits are baked on site. Order loaves or baguettes before 7pm for the following day's picnic.

Great selection of cakes

▶ **Helvellyn Country Kitchen at a glance**

Open: In summer, Tues-Sun and Bank Holiday Mondays, 9am-7pm (check website for winter closures)
Food and specialities: As well as sandwiches, jacket potatoes and burgers, there is a daily specials board; children's menu; full breakfast, including vegetarian option, served until midday
Beverages: Wide range of teas, coffees and soft drinks; also beer and wine
Outside: Patio area in front of café
Dogs: Well-behaved dogs welcome

The Walk

1. Leave the car park, head back to the main road and turn right. Turn right again along a surfaced lane immediately after crossing the bridge over **Glenridding Beck** — signed 'Mires Beck, Helvellyn'. **Helvellyn Country Kitchen** is on the left as you follow the beck upstream. Beyond the first group of buildings, bear left at a fork to start climbing — signed 'Lanty's Tarn'. At the next set of **cottages**, take the path on the left — signed Lanty's Tarn, Helvellyn. The route goes through a gate, swings right through the trees and then heads left as it joins a path from the right. A **stone staircase** winds its way steeply uphill to the woodland edge.

2. The next gate provides access to open, bracken-covered slopes and, as you bear right along the path, you get a superb view across the valley to your right, home to Glenridding Beck. Heron Crag and Glenridding Dodd guard the mouth of the valley on its northern side. The path forks just before another small gate. Bear left here, away from the gate. A handy **bench** at the top of the next rise provides a perfect place to rest and enjoy the beautiful scenery.

3. You soon reach a pair of gates beyond which you can see Lanty's Tarn, a calm stretch of water surrounded by trees. Before you head that way, climb the stile beside the gate just off to the left for a short detour on to **Keldas**, which has a

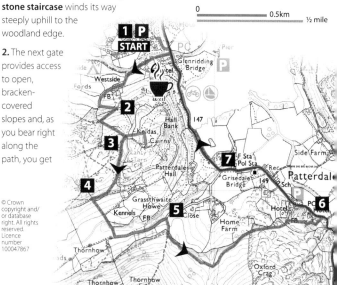

Early morning: *Mist hangs over the Glenridding valley at the start of the walk*

superb outlook over Ullswater. (It's about 550 metres there and back.) Head up the first incline and then bear right at a fork close to a tall, solitary pine. At the top of the next rise, don't be tempted off to the left; instead, bear right to clamber the final 55 metres to the top of this **rocky knoll.** *As well as views of the lake, the pine-covered summit also provides a glimpse of the Helvellyn range.* This is private land with just this one permissive path, so once you've rested, retrace your steps to

the gates near **Lanty's Tarn.** Go through to access this small pool, following the broad path beside the water and then down towards the next valley over — **Grisedale.**

4. Having descended to a wall, you reach a fork marked by a small fingerpost. Bear left here, go through the gate and turn left, heading steeply downhill. The path ends at a gate leading on to a surfaced lane. Turn right — effectively straight on — to cross **Grisedale Beck** in a short while. Keep to the lane when it bends sharp left. Follow

Wonderful viewpoint: *Ullswater seen through the tall Scots pines on Keldas*

it downhill for a further 390 metres. *(To cut the walk short by 1.8 kilometres and avoid the Hag Beck ford, continue along the lane to rejoin the main route by turning left at the junction with the A592 at point 7.)*

5. Go through the large **wooden gate** on the right and follow the path uphill. Just after a **small gate**, turn left at a crossing of ways to follow the clear path through **Glenamara Park**. Having forded **Hag Beck**, keep straight ahead after a gate in a wall. On entering woods

close to the edge of **Patterdale**, bear right at a fork. Turn right on reaching a broad track to drop into **Patterdale**, near the **village shop** and opposite the **White Lion Inn**.

6. Turn left along the **A592**. This road leads all the way back to the car park in Glenridding, about 1.7 kilometres away. There are roadside paths of one sort or another for the entire distance, but you'll need to cross back and forth.

7. A lane leading up into Grisedale on your left marks the point at which those who cut the walk short rejoin the main route. Just after this junction, you'll find

a permissive path through the trees to the right of the road. When this runs out, cross over and pick up a raised path running above the western side of the road. Having dropped back to the road close to **St Patrick's Landing**, cross back over and walk the final few hundred metres into **Glenridding**. The **car park** is on the left just after the road crosses **Glenridding Beck** to complete the walk. ♦

Ice house

Lanty's Tarn was probably named after Lancelot Dobson, whose family once owned much of Grisedale. The natural pool was dammed and enlarged in the nineteenth century by the Marshall family, of Patterdale Hall. They fished here and also dug an ice house into the nearby fellside. In winter, they would cut blocks of ice from the tarn and, using piles of straw and sawdust, store it underground for summer use.

Useful Information

Cumbria Tourism
Cumbria Tourism's official website covers everything from accommodation and events to attractions and adventure. www.golakes.co.uk

Lake District National Park
The Lake District National Park website also has information on things to see and do, plus maps, webcams and news. www.lakedistrict.gov.uk

Tourist Information Centres
The main TICs provide free information on everything from accommodation and travel to what's on and walking advice.

Ambleside	01539 432 582	tic@thehubofambleside.com
Bowness	01539 442 895	bownesstic@lake-district.gov.uk
Coniston	01539 441 533	mail@conistontic.org
Keswick	01768 772 645	keswicktic@lake-district.gov.uk
Penrith	01768 867 466	pen.tic@eden.gov.uk
Ullswater	01768 482 414	ullswatertic@lake-district.gov.uk
Windermere	01539 446 499	windermeretic@southlakeland.gov.uk

Cumbrian tea shops and cafés
There are dozens of tea shops and cafés scattered throughout the Lake District National Park, with more opening every season. They range from simple places, such as Low Bridge End Farm at St John's-in-the-Vale, offering hot drinks and home-made cakes on a self-service and honesty box system, to more sophisticated outlets serving up the latest superfood salads alongside gourmet burgers and vegan meals.

The growth in the numbers of tea shops and cafés has been accompanied by a rise in the number of local, artisan beverage suppliers, particularly of coffee. At last count, there were at least eight independent roasters in Cumbria.

Visit www.thecoffeeroasters.co.uk for details of artisan roasters in Cumbria and around the UK.

Weather
Five-day forecast for the Lake District
0844 846 2444   www.lakedistrict.gov.uk/weatherline